The Beach, C.

.

# The Beach, C.

2018 - 2021

The full name of my creativity coach Sara,
is Sara Saltee.

ISBN  978-1-716-27785-6

available at lulu.com
written under pseudonym LS Harteveld
cover photo Stinson Beach by Adam Derewecki

www.lsharteveld.nl
Twitter @LSHarteveld

*It's a love story.*
*~Sharon Stone*

# 1

## Fear got me thinking I was anything less than Basic Instinct's Catherine Tramell

I've been fascinated with Catherine Tramell from the moment she appeared on the screen.

And then I'm not counting the opening scene of Basic Instinct, where a naked, anonymous blonde with the same breasts as Sharon Stone murders a retired rock 'n' roll star and we're supposed to assume that was her, but the first time we see her face.

This is after detective Nick Curran and his partner Gus have arrived to the beach house of a sexy as hell, blonde, millionaire writer (!!) to ask her where she was the night of the murder.

"How long were you dating him?" Nick asks.

"I wasn't dating him," Catherine Tramell answers. "I was fucking him."

Mind blown!

It was 1992.

I was twenty and in a steady relationship because of two reasons. One was that I wanted to lose my virginity and secure having a good and steady sex life after.

And the other reason I chose a steady relationship was because I got such bad anxiety attacks from giving oral sex without a condom, because I was so afraid of hiv/aids, that staying single and at risk was definitely not an option anymore.

I had enough of nights trembling alone in my bed, afraid to tell anyone why I was so afraid. I had obviously put myself at risk by doing that and now I could get really sick and nobody was going to love me anymore.

I had a deep understanding that I wasn't strong enough, or tough enough to deal with that shit.

So at seventeen I threw in the towel, and went steady.

*Like a normal person.*

Except that a normal person would probably not see Basic Instinct about ten times in cinema (there was a time when they ran it for 2.50 per ticket).

Not rent the VHS a couple of times, at a time when they didn't have their own player and had to rent that as well.

Not buy a Basic Instinct dvd as soon as they had a dvd player and then to top it all off, buy Basic Instinct 2 on dvd as well.

Together with three other people ☺

Those were signs that something was up underneath the good girl "facade". Facade obviously doesn't stand for that I would cheat. It's actually surprisingly easy to stay faithful if you think cheating will get you killed.

Facade means that everything in my teens had been about me loving sex so much, but also the thrill of being in love, and with new men, and clothes that come off for the first time.

Nothing in me had dreamed or longed for a long term relationship, aside for the longing to put an end to the anxiety attacks.

It was all so obvious.

In hindsight.

Because in 1992, I was absolutely certain I had zero in common with Catherine Tramell, except the farfetched wish that I had been anything like her.

Wouldn't that be awesome!

*"I wasn't dating him. I was fucking him."*

Man, that would be worth a million, to be that emotionally contained. But I knew I wasn't, and I just focused on her style of clothing, adopted some of that. Which I still do till this day. I always wear white long coats, only wear uni (never print), and my entire wardrobe consists of black, white, grey, beige, dark blue, every flavor pink, and bright red. That's it.

Aside from pink and red, those are all Catherine Tramell colors, and smooth fabrics.

In Basic Instinct 2 they gave her two furry coats. One dark brown, one green. I immediately was all like:

"She would never wear that!"

Maybe the stylist of Basic Instinct 2 went on maternity leave and somebody else stepped in, but it looked totally out of character. Maybe the critics were right it was a bad movie.

Later on, when I became a writer, I sometimes presented myself as Catherine Tramell, by using stills from the movies. But for me it was more tongue in cheek. Surely nobody would think I was that sassy, that chic or anything like her.

Because although I have learned to manage my fear of hiv/aids, to a degree where I actually could have a life where I fuck people, not date them, my sexual orientation turned out to be a little bit different than Miss Tramell's.

Because I'm a monogamist: I like to have only one lover, one pair of hands touching me, one dick to give blowjobs to.

Thinking I would ever go around having multiple lovers, was more an idea that stemmed from thinking that was simply how a sexually free woman would live. And how I would live too, I assumed, if I didn't have all that fear holding me back.

That image, or ideal, had nothing to do with who I was and what really made me tick. I know now that for me one partner is ideal. If I ever fall in love with two men at the same time, I'll up my game. But me preferring one partner doesn't have anything to do with fear anymore.

Because something else about my arrangement, is very exciting. Not to say nerve wrecking.

And although I speak very little of this – as if I'm so worried that only confessing I feel this way, and that it does scare me, and that I don't have anxiety attacks yet but that I can feel the layer of calm and collected is so very thin – is this:

I am a secret mistress and that might get me killed.

After more than three years, and working through a ton of inner stuff, I *own* being secret mistress.

I'm not ashamed of it.

I have many things to tell about it and I wouldn't have it any other way.

And yet... I cannot stop being scared that this could cost me my life. Either by social exclusion or literally, because someone wants revenge.

I know my lover will leave me.

No way he could afford standing up for me, when all hell breaks loose. He would have to choose her side, even if she does give him his appropriate punishment of whatever she thinks he deserves. But nobody will take it out on him.

They will project that on me.

Because *somebody* has to pay for the betrayal of his wife. And it only takes *one* person with aggression issues who thinks that way.

That thought sickens me to my stomach.

Like I said, I could easily flip into having anxiety attacks over this. And I'm currently planning out how I want to proceed with my writing career:

If I want publicity yes or no.

If I want a regular publisher yes or no.

If I want to even be known in the Netherlands, or if I want to immediately focus entirely on the English market? Or is that decision based on fear for the Dutch market? Fear of getting killed for my ideas? And if it's based on fear, then is it a bad thing?

Those are my thoughts.

And I actually considered, and I haven't told this to anyone, to end my relationship..

To stop being a secret mistress.

And to say: "Yes, I was a secret mistress, but when I realized I had to choose between telling my story and risking my life, or staying quiet, I ended it. I am more a writer than a lover."

That's legit.

And it *would* take the sharpest edges of my mistress status, and of the hatred that it could trigger, since I would now be an ex-mistress. Except it would not be *me* any more than locking myself up in long term relationships from age seventeen to thirty-four was. I was hiding from the real me then, because I couldn't deal with the threat of death and social exclusion.

And I was considering running now, either from my career as a writer, or from my relationship, because I couldn't deal with the threat of death and social exclusion now.

It was exactly the same scenario and the sequel was not becoming a particularly good movie.

Until I realized something that my lover, this lover that I have now, pointed out to me at the beginning of our relationship.

I informed him about my fear of std's, but we also fantasized together about sex that was really exciting and didn't fit into the warm, cuddly, intimate corner of sexuality.

There wasn't anything we didn't both look forward to test out, play out, dive right in.

We were a match made in heaven and I had finally found someone willing to play at my level of desired sexual tension.

"No wonder you need this," he said, after we had spoken of yet another thing that would be a very hard limit in most relationships. "You grew up being so scared of aids. It was so filled with tension. Unless the pressure is dialed up, you don't feel a thing."

In all those years, I had never looked at it that way.
But of course, he was right.

I've always had, perhaps "unsettling" is the best word, sexual fantasies, but the aids phobia certainly amplified it. From that moment on I would always associate sex with risk. The only time I didn't, was in my long term relationships. We had great sex but I only felt the thrill, I only felt truly alive the first couple of months.
Then it died.

Everything after that didn't move me to my core, because I knew I was safe. The tagline, or subtitle of Basic Instinct 2 is *Risk Addiction*. It is explained when a psychiatrist evaluates Catherine Tramell for her trial:
Psychiatrist: "Her behavior is driven by what we call a risk addiction. A compulsive need to prove to herself that she can take risks. And survive dangers others can't."
Judge: "Why would a person do that?"
Psychiatrist: "The greater the risk, the greater the proof of her omnipotence. Her existence, really."

I know that my current relationship, as a secret mistress of someone who totally supports me in my sexual fantasies, is the best thing that ever happened to me. I am so happy I found him, and that we have a relationship form that will always push me, and test me, and yes it frightens the shit out of me.
I still don't know how to balance the risks of fame or speaking up for my sexual orientation.
But I do know that I need risks in order to "get it up".

That I will ever be satisfied having sex the way normal people do, is an illusion.
Judge: "When you say she has a risk addiction, is this condition likely to get worse?"

Psychiatrist: "I think the only thing that'd stop her, I suspect the only limit for her, would be her own death."

*Fear got me thinking I was anything less than Basic Instinct's Catherine Tramell*
was written on 8 May 2018

# 2
## Who's that Girl?

*Quitting her career in yoga,*
*has left Lauren craving for some guidance on who she really is.*
*And she's in for a surprise.*

This is how it's going to be.
A new start. A new me.
And a different way to write: On my offline computer which is two decades old.
But my God does this feel good.

I often compare the different stages of my life, my emotional states, to feeling sick. Right before you throw up it's the worst of the worst. But then after you vomit you feel so relieved and you think:
"That was it already?"
Or maybe if you're more poetic you prefer the saying:
The darkest hour is right before the dawn.

My darkest hour was indeed before the dawn, although it's been two weeks now. My decision to quit my business was followed by 48 hours of disintegration. Like Brad Pitt's transformation in Interview with the Vampire:
He fell into a state that was somewhere between a psychotic delirium, and coming down from crack. Before he was reborn a vampire.
And before I was reborn a writer.
More beautiful, stronger, and living on different things.
That's how I was reborn, all fresh and new.
Just that Brad Pitt seemed to be more stable!

"That's because in reality we move in and out of seeing the vision of our new life," my coach Sara said. "Sometimes it's foggy."

But the weirdest thing is forgetting to tap into it.
ALL you have to do to feel better is see the future: Just to lift your head and look straight ahead.
Yet instead I've been looking down a lot lately.

Although it's not all negative. It seems to be my way of letting go of the old, and preparing for the new alike. I do this by going through all my stuff, and my archives in particular.
Even the admin I've neglected since July, which was when I realized reorganizing my business was not going to be as smooth as I thought it would be. And that maybe I didn't want any of it, anymore. That messy box of archived admin, that had been accumulating for the last months, was suddenly appealing to go through. And I've also cleared out my yoga stuff.
Everything that was part of my past, my job, my identity.

I even realized my initial love for yoga, which started in 1998, was never going to come back. It was just a dream that quitting teaching would magically turn back the clock and restore yoga to what I perceived it to be, before I took an official training.
After twenty years yoga had died on me.
I got inspired to start cycling. Which was actually my form of exercise pre-yoga, as well as pre-gym.
From my 12th to my 18th I cycled to school. Two forty minute bike rides. And it kept me a small size 6.
The only reason I started gaining weight in my late teens was because I started doing fitness. It was all muscle.
So now I'm taking hour long bike rides.

I told my coach Sara that I feel sadder about losing my business, than about losing yoga. And she specified that it was the freedom teaching yoga had brought me. It had allowed me ample time to write. Now there were two ways in which I could continue being a writer: Either I could get a real job.

And this would discharge me from creating content, being active on social media, selling books, promoting myself. I could focus fully on creative writing, and didn't have to do any of the business stuff. OR

I could invest that time I would normally spend with an employer, running my own business. And start making money as a writer. I was definitely all for option 2. At the very least, before I would assume I couldn't make a living from writing books.

Sara made a suggestion.

And she did it as if it was something I could be taking the wrong way. Like a lewd, indecent proposal.

"In order to hold this vision, some people – and I have no idea if this speaks to you – but they make like a collage. Of where they want to go."

"You mean a vision board!" I yelled.

Sara was not too keen on using that word but yes. A vision board. "I'll be right back Sara!" I shouted at our Zoom connection as I rushed out of my study. I came back with my vision board, that I had in my bed room. I had refreshed it a few days ago.

Eager to show her that I had been very active, I started to explain all the things on it.

Such as a daily schedule which included sleeping in;

An hour of soothing archiving and sorting through clippings; Daily housekeeping which I found the most powerful mindset work imaginable. I actually used the words "mental spa"!

And the schedule contained second breakfast.

"I think every schedule should include second breakfast," I said to Sara. "It's probably the most important meal of the day. Mine is French toast."

I was still dreaming of how beautiful life is, if you can have daily French toast at ten. (eggy bread in UK English, and *wentelteefjes* in Dutch) when Sara said she now understood even better why I didn't have a desire to learn how to write.

Nor a desire to read, in order to become a better writer.

She had already explained to me that there were so many types of writers. From marketing writers to text book writers. So that it was a broad term.

But I told her, that although I knew that, I was still shocked by how many writers, who I did or had considered like-minded souls, were concerned with learning how to write.

I was of the opinion that a real writer needed to UNLEARN, undo, to go back to the ultimate basics of keeping life as simple as possible. Not cram your mind with what others think, have written, or anything. I was a firm believer in uneducating yourself, and taking in as little writing or opinions of others as you could. It baffled me that every writer I knew, seemed to disagree!

They were all keen to get approved by readers, publishers, critics. And they spent their lives getting better at the skill of writing.

Yet I was a hundred percent convinced I was right.

And I would never change my mind.

A writer's job was to not pay attention to anything but their inner world. Where my mind now drifted back to how sweet life was when your second breakfast consisted of French toast.

"I have mine with lots of sugar and cinnamon, Sara," I brought the conversation back to what really made me tick. Apparently even talking about learning how to write drained me.

"They're so good! And I bake them in real butter. Lots of it."

Sara smiled and she tried to bring my attention back to what she had discovered on my vision board. Next to my ideal day, it contained a poster I had created that said *Sleep yourself thin*;

A collage of photos of me, or that inspired me, all taken in London. And it held two A4 laminated posters, both with the header "365 days", and each had about ten photos of Sharon Stone, playing the stunning and most likely murderous Catherine Tramell, in Basic Instinct 2.

Mysterious and not to be trusted. This is who I really am.

"Basic Instinct 2 was also filmed in London," I told Sara, explaining the connection between all the photos. "Three people saw that movie. Including me."
And then I started telling Sara that the entirely fictional character of novelist Catherine Tramell from Basic Instinct 1 and 2, was my writer idol. Because she was just soo wicked!
And well dressed.

"She's so mysterious!" I yelled. "And she can NOT be trusted, Sara!"
As if Sara would run into Catherine on her way to the grocery store.

Sara kept pointing at my board.
"That's not a typical writer's board," she said.
Which surprised me. I had never thought about it like that. I didn't even know what a typical writer's board would look like..
"There are no people there sitting at their desks. Typing."
Sara was right. There weren't.

And in over a decade, I had never owned any vision board that contained those things. Nor had my vision board ever had pictures of real life writers, nor any pictures of books. Nothing like that. I agreed with Sara that it was indeed odd that my vision board didn't hold anything related to writing.
"You're more like a performance artist," Sara said. "That's why you need to be alone and why you spend so much time cleaning your house and sorting through all your things.
You need to clear the way, so that you can be in that energy of being

mysterious.
The energy of being that person."

What Sara was telling me was that I had never quit my yoga studio to set up my career in writing.
But to become intriguing, fascinating, and Someone Who Cannot Be Trusted.
More beautiful.
Stronger.

And living on different things.

*Who's that Girl?*
was written on 19 October 2018

# 3
# Being Catherine Tramell (Basic Instinct)

I didn't even have to upload a photo for this post.
I could pick one from the previous posts because I've been writing about Sharon Stone's woman in white (directly inspired by Hitchcock's Vertigo) for as long as I can remember.
And it's like this thing where an insight, a certain knowledge about yourself, just keeps sinking in deeper.
Ever since 1992.

I saw the movie countless of times in the 90s already, because a few years after its release they started replaying it at a discount theater. I own the DVD and recently bought a new copy of Basic Instinct 2, because I had lost the first one. That's how important Catherine Tramell is to me; I need that collection in order.
My identification with Catherine Tramell has turned out to be this exponential thing.

In the beginning, it seemed like not much was happening. Like a flat line where I just "hit" the mark, every time I went to see it. But without seeing much development.
Then I started dressing like her.
The 90s was the first decade where I bought white, khaki and camel clothing, including turtle necks and over-the-hip woolen coats.

But it wasn't until the release of Basic Instinct 2 that the graph started taking off.
Fourteen years after I had been a university student in her early twenties captivated by Catherine Tramell, the thought that there had been more than just the clothing that had kept me glued to the screen,

started evolving.
Something that she did. With men.
With the world.
Their fear.
Her power.

It had been a deception that there were no similarities between us. And they were rooted in feeling vulnerable rather than powerful.
Because I am an emphatic, loving person.

I can't pass a beggar without giving money or a starving bee without feeding him. I over-deliver, give immediate refunds and I don't steal in any way, shape or form. I cannot remember I ever tried to hurt someone by being unkind without (from my point of view) that person starting first and it being self-defense.
I consider myself an emotional pushover, bound to her inner moral compass. I simply laugh when someone wonders if they can trust me, because my own moral code will exceed any expectations set by society.

My mistake, the reason it took me for over a decade before I understood that the similarities between me and Catherine Tramell were greater than a love for white coats, was that I assumed my own moral compass was something the world could see.
I still don't know why they don't, but very few do.
And the ones who do are usually very easygoing, friendly people.
Who say: "You're so sweet, thank you."
or
"You're so social, you really see people."

They're the very people who (I think) should have been afraid of me, if there had been anything dangerous or ill-willing about me. They're the ones who see my goodness.

And then my heart just breaks open.
Because no one ever says that.

I feel I've been criticized for everything. From the shoes I wear to how I express myself, to the way I handle criticism then conveniently called feedback.

Yet because of the inner-compass I didn't identify as the strong woman Catherine Tramell, who was mostly only referred to as a serial killer. Not a saver of Californian bees.

What I failed to see was that to the outside world I was Catherine Tramell.

The hostility, impatience and determination to find something wrong with me has been such a perpetual part of my surroundings, I cannot remember the time I didn't try to offer some kind of excuse for myself. I'll probably be diagnosed as autistic in 2020 which is great but I'm just happy that something will come out of that psychological testing. If I can hold up a label "autistic" or "borderline" or "narcissism"? People will feel satisfied that they "felt something was wrong with me" and move on.

I hope I don't have a high IQ because that will be useless in getting on people's good or even neutral side.

If all they find wrong with me is being gifted I really have no other option than taking "the Catherine Tramell route".

There is genius in what she does.

In both of the movies we don't actually see her (identified by seeing her face) killing people.

It is implied, but everything could also be explained as being an accident, someone else impersonating her, or otherwise wanting it to look like she did it.

As much as part 2 (2006) differs from part 1 (1992); That is identical. You don't know if she really did it.

And in both movies she plays with people's fear for her and messes with their minds. Where I have spent my entire life trying to defend myself to fit in, explaining myself – and getting absolutely nowhere with the whole thing except in a state of not-belonging;

She just lets them have it.

She successfully passes lie-detector tests, turns ten-to-one interrogation scenes around, gets her psychiatrist to break all his own rules and drives men into obsessively and compulsively wanting her. The creators of the movie, never questioned that ultimately she was the one who did it.

She was evil.

When in reality, 27 years into living in a defensive, non-Catherine Tramell way, I can testify that she didn't have a real choice. That even if she wasn't a serial killer at all, had excused for herself, and for the impact she had on people?

Even if she had carefully tiptoed around every ego of every psychiatrist or every detective?

They would have found something wrong with her.

A way to put it all on her.

*psychiatrist:*
*"Washburn thinks that you slit Denise's throat.*

*Catherine:*
*"Me? You're the one that hated her.*
*Maybe I'm acting out your unconscious impulses."*

*psychiatrist:*
*"Stop it!"*

*Catherine:*
*"Do you think it's possible that you want me to be the killer?"*

We don't know if Catherine really did it. And we don't even know if she might have been saving bees or gave money to the homeless. All we know is that people saw her as being guilty.

And she never made an attempt to prove them wrong.

Saved her 27 years.

*Being Catherine Tramell (Basic Instinct)*
was written on 26 October 2019

# 4
## Back to Basics

*This is a letter to my creativity coach Sara Saltee.*
*Before our coaching call, I always give her a headsup.*

Dear Sara,

Have I ever started a letter with:
"Dear Sara, I fucked up?"
Because if I haven't, then I would like to open with that now.

And it's not because I was "on the wrong track" or anything like it.
More that the right track brought things I did not expect and wasn't ready for.
But good news first!

My hunch to FULLY go with the Basic Instinct/ Catherine Tramell vibe of things, was right and is very fulfilling. I know I'm on the right path/ was on the right path during our last call when you exclaimed:
"You're sitting just like her! You see?"
Fully leaning back, arms dangling loosely on the sides. I see it, Sara! I've been sitting like that a lot.

And I've extracted my notes on consent play from a notebook I had been keeping, with the intention of writing (manually) a book.
But I'm going to type my consent play notes out, and put a new perspective on it.
Write a new ending, or perhaps a new introductory chapter.

Where I conclude that I can't write a book on consent play, because that is not what I have with my lover.

Or had maybe, because I haven't seen him in months.
What we have is so special, not so much because of the power play or consent play during sex;
It is in the complexity of our play when we're not in bed.

Exactly the way the relationship between former-undercover-agent-turned-detective Nick Curran (Michael Douglas) and million dollar writer with a double major in psychology and English lit, Catherine Tramell (Sharon Stone), is way more about how they interact outside of bed, than about the way they behave between the sheets.

And there's so much nuance to their performance. So much complexity.

The major mind-fuck of Basic Instinct (1992) is that there are two coexisting story lines, both with a different killer. Like the drawing of the young girl and the old woman: They're both there.
One doesn't exclude the other.

Yet the director Paul Verhoeven insists the movie ultimately portrays Catherine as the killer.
That for him it is totally clear who did it.
And all the critics echoed his perspective, without further investigating it, but 27 years later I rewatched this movie a couple of times and I see three things.


1. God, Michael Douglas is hot.

Every time he has seen Catherine, he walks taller, he's totally self-assured and absolutely irresistible. And he plays his cards with her well, too.
He likes talking with her, because she plays him at his level.

But it's especially his tooth pick chewing smirk, after he has spent the night at her place and now meets his friend Gus again, that is absolutely golden.

"You fucked her!" Gus exclaims.

"Goddamn dumb sonofabitch... You fucked her! Goddamn, you are one dumb sonofabitch –"

Well, he's not of course.

A dumb son of a bitch I mean.

He's very smart to have recognized that she's the only one who can give him the thrill he had working undercover, combined with being the fuck of the century.

As is his explicit appreciation of their encounter.

Which brings me to Catherine.

The second thing I saw this time around:

2. Catherine's so kind and sweet

Go watch that movie in 2019 and tell me you're not taken by her sassy remarks, her broad honest smile and her intense sorrow when her best friend is killed.

Sure, she's ruthless with the five cops who try to interrogate her. She makes them uncomfortable to the bone. But she does it by lighting a cigarette, not wearing underwear, and correcting them when they ask her why she needs a white scarf to tie people up, when she liked men to use their hands.

Catherine: "That's not what I said."

cop: "No?"

Catherine: "No. I said I liked Johnny, to use his hands."

She outsmarts all of them.
Which brings me to the last thing I saw.


3. She's too smart to be the killer

Paul Verhoeven said she did it. All the critics said she did it. Every page or blog dedicated to Basic Instinct will say she did it. But she didn't do it.
It wouldn't make sense.

Why would someone who likes to play games, and likes to manipulate people, get her hands dirty with something as blunt and ugly as killing people when they're harmless?
There is no fun.

And I think this interpretation of Basic Instinct is made possible because Sharon Stone herself, gave the role its intellectual baggage. Back in the 90s, she was the first one I heard of, who came out as highly intelligent and a member of Mensa.

I think what happened is that although she stuck to the script, you could feel the depth and intelligence of her. The intelligence of Catherine Tramell became so real, that although the script had intended her to be the killer:
It doesn't make any sense anymore.
In a way, they hired an actress that was too smart for their own good.
To this day Paul Verhoeven and everybody else might say she did it.

When I tell you:
Every Mensa member will see that movie, and know that she didn't.

And if only, IF ONLY, I had spent two weeks doing nothing else than analyzing Basic Instinct: But I didn't.
I went on a different path as well.

And I will like "management-summary" you through it, although that's technically not a verb, but here's what happened:
I am still convinced that my meltdown, and current problems are related to what others would call, and what "science" calls: Autism.

This means that I have no interest in an entire layer of communication, which the majority of the world's population requires in order to be able to interact with you, and that I wear a mask interacting with them.
A mask which I switch, depending on who I have in front of me.

Now I had already determined that agreeable, cooperative Lauren, would be replaced by the Catherine Tramell mask, for one-offs, and all short and medium sized interactions with the exclusion of friends and family and people I wanted to be nice to.
Not just to save me the energy of bending over backwards, but also because my ice queen mask was a much better representation of what people tend to feel in my presence.
A white coat and platinum blond hair, would be a better mirror of the discomfort they felt, than my "normal person" mask.

In an ideal world I would go for koala imitations and third person Elmo language, but I think this would be even more confusing. And only fellow "autistics" would be able to appreciate having communication take place on a whole different plane of reality.
So Catherine Tramell would just have to do.

But this fine tuning on my masking strategies, wasn't going to solve my problems with regard to not being able to work, and my suicidal thoughts and possible other mental health issues.
And in my search for answers, I was sucked deeper into the diagnoses.

Every day there was a deeper understanding, that I qualify, perhaps even over-qualify, on the criteria for autism as they have been defined in the latest DSM in 2011.

Before that, I would have Asperger's. Which in common tongue no longer qualified as a psychiatric condition, but as pleasantly mad and interesting.
For 25 years Asperger's had a special position within the realm of mental disorders, and so did the patients who had it.

But ever since Asperger's has been dropped, and only autism remains, everybody newly diagnosed should say (correctly): "I am autistic" or "I have autism".
Not "I have Asperger's"

Now it's not that I have a problem with calling myself autistic.
But the trouble is: Others do.

The stigma surrounding autism is so heavy that the mental burden that comes with it, is for me, a sensitive undiagnosed Aspie, who knows she's an Aspie because she loves to go out and have fun with other Aspies, is just too much.
Especially after two years on an erratic slope downhill.

I wrote an in-depth piece on the matter; *Goodbye to autism. Plus a new way to greet each other*.
It's like my "meta" as we geeks call such a thing, on the entire history of Asperger's from the 30s to current day.
And my declaration of why I can't keep going on.
Why I have no choice but to cut myself out of the autistic loop.

Now what I did not say there was what I am going to do to get better.
And to get the best help.
And Hans Asperger the discoverer of Asperger would have approved

because 50 years after his research on autism which included feisty little boys who constantly challenged him, and whom he called Little Professors;
Asperger confessed he made a mistake.

That these boys didn't have autism, they were highly gifted.
EXACTLY where I am going to start.
How do I move from here if I am highly gifted?

I had a conversation with an amazing researcher and therapist, whose singular mission seems to be to save people from getting an autism diagnosis, and getting them to a therapist or coach specialized in highly gifted people instead.

Because I recognize myself in the complex, imaginative, play of the highly gifted Little Professors. And in Hans Asperger's observation that the only way to tell them to do something was by addressing them like equals, show no personal interest in the result, and separate the message from the messenger.

For example, you could ask:
"What's on your schedule today?
Not: "I want you to do this and this."

The moment the boys could sense that Hans was emotionally invested they would start taunting Hans.
I fully recognize myself in that dynamic.

You have to intrigue and seduce me.
Like my lover intrigues and seduces me.
And like Michael Douglas intrigues and seduces Catherine.
The parents and school teachers of the Little Professors had not been able to do that. They thought they could get away treating them like

normal kids.

They were wrong.

Men have thought they could keep my interest without making an effort to intrigue and seduce me.

That never worked.

And the five cops in the interrogation room thought their presence would intimidate Catherine Tramell. And instead she wiped the floor with them.

A few days ago Sharon Stone received the GQ woman of the year award, and she gave a speech commemorating her life changing moment when she crossed her legs.

It was not an easy to follow speech.

And just like the movie there seemed to be multiple ways to interpret it. But one sentence stood out, because of its simplicity:

"We have every right to be powerful, in whatever form of sexuality we choose to have."

The times that I wanted to know the "truth" about autism or my mind are over. All the wandering in the dark, thinking about what is wrong with me. Getting lost into the cave searching for the truth. Behind every corner a new one. Just one more and I'll be there.

Just one more.

I will never be there.

And with every corner turned, I lose more energy, I lose myself.

I lose.

Two weeks after finding myself in Catherine Tramell pose, video chatting with you on our coaching call, I had managed to entirely fuck it up and lose it all.

The video from Sharon Stone was like a gift from heaven.
It was Friday, a friend sent it to me.
And it felt like a little nudge from heaven:
"Hey Lauren! Put on your white dress, pull your hair up, and go find that man of yours. All this heaviness, it just ain't you."

Maybe that's the ultimate reason I know I will never go down that path of getting an autism diagnosis, ever again. Because although this didn't bother me the first few months, over the last week I just couldn't find my sexuality anymore.
I had lost it looking for the truth on autism.

Sharon Stone added something, after telling us we all have our right to our own unique sexuality. And it was the thing that brought it home, just in case you managed to miss it.
She said:
"We have every right to be powerful, in whatever form of sexuality we choose to have."
And then:
"And no one is allowed to take that away from you."

No one, Sara.


~Lauren
*An Unexamined life Is Not Worth living*




*Back to Basics*
was written on 11 November 2019

# 5

## Rocket Queen

from A Letter From A Stranger, 1994

2 November 1994

If I tell you what I've been up to, you will just laugh your socks off at my ignorance.

That I ever thought fall 1994, would be the time when I would write a groundbreaking book on consent play within unconventional and highly exciting relationships between dare I say "superior" minds. I haven't heard from my lover Bear for ages, and I would not be surprised if he is with another woman, probably a less problematic one.

So I've already been punished for my arrogance of calling us superior minds.

On the bright side, since I'm already in pain, this does entitle me to start speaking my truth because I'm no longer promoting a success lifestyle here.

The current situation immediately illustrates the drawbacks of being so demanding in your love life.

If it works, this relationship style will bring you the best thing you ever got, the best thing he ever got, and in all likeliness the best thing anybody going back three generations on both sides ever got. But most likely it will not work and you'll end up totally alone and everybody will believe you totally deserved it.

And I probably did.

You know what the problem is, aside from having pictured life differently than feeling old and terribly underused at age 22?

That once you've gotten used to playing at the level Bear and me did, there is just no way you're ever going back.
If he wants a normal family life with someone else, or a woman who will inspire him to be monogamous?
Then I will not get in the way.

And I've already proven that because every time he fell out of communication or put me on the back burner like now when we see each other once every three months or so; I stay exactly where I am. I don't approach him to see where we stand or, more precisely, to ask him where I stand.

I don't make plans to end it and get someone else instead.

The only repeating pattern is that his absence makes me realize it would be better to have multiple lovers, because it's just not ideal to have so little sex.
But owning my Miss Arrogance Catherine Tramell Basic Instinct persona:
Who says other people have sex this good?
Or a relationship this exciting?

Whenever I think not hearing from Bear is my cue to take action and start dating, or at least actively entertain the thought of getting a second lover (one equally good) it doesn't happen.
And when I started writing this book on consent play, I originally thought it was limited to what Bear and me did between the sheets. Consent play would define as sex where I play I am the victim of some sort of abuse, to put it bluntly.

And I don't think the word "play" does it justice, because it's best known as a term in S&M, which is something entirely different from consent play.
For multiple reasons none of which I will get into.

But "play" also makes us sound like really bad actors when our words, each and every one of them, are improvised and meant to arouse and increase pleasure, both of ourselves and the other.
We are at different levels of reality, and we play/talk/act on these different levels, at the same time.

There is our real life selves, who are the main thing.
Our normal conversation is still part of what we do, especially for quick check-ins.
And then there is our play connection.

This can be singular, where we really deliberately play out one fantasy.
But more often it's an improvised scene, something one of us initiates, and two or more concepts of consent play could be covered in one session.

Finally there is the connection based on our past as well as our future selves.
Memories of what we did in the past, or things we'd like to do in the future.
Fantasies like "How would you like it if one day.."

These multi-leveled sexual encounters were absolutely mind blowing compared to anything I ever had ever done with any other man.
But because I was still a virgin when we started out, I didn't think much of it.
I assumed that all people must be doing this.

It wasn't until after a few years that I began to understand how lucky I had been.
I had asked Bear to make love to me, just once, because I knew he could do it (he was a player) and I was a virgin and wanted it to be done right.
When someone like that sticks around, it takes a while before you

understand most men would not have been comfortable being asked so directly for sex, nor would they have stuck around to discover your sexuality, and find the magical match where you (the girl) likes to be taken against her will and he (Bear) likes to do that.

So because of my relative inexperience, it had taken me a while to realize that Bear was worth his weight in gold.

A few weeks ago, I decided it was a good time to write the consent play thing down, since I didn't seem to have a sex life anymore.
It could serve as a guide for others but also for myself if I ever wanted a new man.
Having a manifesto on my first real relationship, would make sure I preserved what I had learned, make it my own.
Even if Bear would no longer want to see me, I would live on as the woman I became because of him.
Which was not the sexless, worker bee shadow of a woman, I had become.

Late at night, before I went to sleep, I started writing in a journal.
It wasn't the best time to write, but at least it was the last thing I did before I went to sleep.
Something that nourished me on a soul level regardless of how bland my life was.
But things turned sour when I started discussing our relationship style with friends.
Why I appreciated Bear so much, and found it difficult to picture myself meeting someone that was "up for it".

I discovered a discrepancy between what I want from a man, and what seems to be accepted as normal.
It was impossible to explain what Bear and me have, without challenging their beliefs.

Here are some of the beliefs I encountered in others when I tried to explain my current (or perhaps past?) relationship with Bear:

1. A belief that monogamy is a trade-off

There seems to be the misconception that because Bear has other women "I can do whatever I want.", implying to have sex with other men.
Yes, I can have sex with whomever I want.
As can you and you and you and everybody in their right mind.

However, I don't like men touching me with whom I don't have a long-term understanding.
The initial one-off with Bear was a necessary evil because I wanted to lose my virginity and didn't want to claim him.

The reason Bear is my only lover is because so far he is the only man I am in love with and with whom I have matching sexual preferences.
My fidelity is not because I feel I owe it to him, nor because I believe monogamy is the morally right thing to do.
It just comes as a natural consequence of the current situation and my preferences.

As does the other side of the coin:

2. They believe someone who cheats/ has multiple partners is not serious and uncommitted

The reason I often let this pass, is because I don't want to come off as if I'm trying to prove that Bear loves me.
I don't know what I mean to him and maybe he is uncommitted and

not serious, who knows.
And who even cares?

I think my biggest problem with this insatiable urge to know if someone is serious, as in aspiring a life-long monogamous pairing, is because I find it of no value.

What I value is:
What does someone do to make our time together unforgettable? And I do not mean any planning going out for the day, which is not as good as deciding in the moment itself.

Bear and me both show up clean, interested, funny, laid-back, trusting, good-humored.
To me to then start investigating if someone is serious, is as if you're pissing in your own drink.

Don't piss in your own drink.


3. They believe a good sexual match is;
Irrelevant compared to the other parts of your relationship, or;
That good sex is sheer luck, or last option;
Good sex is a natural consequence of liking each other.
All wrong.

This was really the point where I stopped working on my book about consent play, because I realized it all starts by making sex the main event in your relationship, in your life.
Something you are going to facilitate and make a top priority.

Something to be taken into account with every move you make, and every decision as a couple:

"Is this beneficial, or detrimental to my/ our sex life?"

That it is absolutely impossible to aspire having a normal looking relationship on the outside, and enjoy meaningful, layered consent play in private.

So in the end consent play, wasn't a sexual preference at all;
It was a relationship style!
It was the game we play when we're *not* in bed.

The constant tension of not knowing if I will ever see him again, was what made me such a big fan of our play.
Any man wanting to know where our relationship was going, or wanting me to take responsibility for his feelings, for his life, was not going to get anywhere with me.
Our mysterious undefined relationship, had been a prerequisite in order to do the consent play I intended to write about.

If I wanted to write a book that would serve the world, it had to be on the relationship style itself, which I found a totally boring topic.
I didn't want to write an entirely boring book.
But it was this relationship style, which me and Bear had accidentally invented, which was the basis for the great sex life.

The consent play had been the most remarkable aspect of what we did.
And it was the aspect that got confused with S&M a lot, and partly because of that I had been so motivated to write an entire pleasure guide on consent play and how to do it.
But I knew now that our consent play would never have existed without that Catherine Tramell, Nick Curran, Basic Instinct relationship style.

And with Bear gone, not a lover in sight, and my self-esteem reaching new lows after every workweek, there was nothing left to write about.

I need to get my act together and start doing what I had set out to do, the moment I started writing in that journal late at night. The real reason behind me claiming the level Bear and I had reached, was so that I would be able to keep it, long after he had left.

I had hoped the writing would help me to become the strong woman I used to be.

But I was wrong because it was never in my writing, it was in me. Or it had been, because "it" wasn't anymore.

I need to start remembering.

Start becoming.

Start embodying that bold virgin that asked him for an encounter over coffee, at a cafe December 1989.

The young woman with whom he went to the movies, seeing Basic Instinct, in 1992. Several times.

And how we somehow knew we'd be the only people in that audience who would understand that this wasn't about if she had done it. That Basic Instinct was about Catherine Tramell's and Nick Curran's desire to live an exciting life.

A life no one would understand.

Bear may have returned to his normal life, but that should never again be a reason for me to stop being Catherine Tramell.

*Rocket Queen*
from "A letter from a stranger" (diary 1994-1996)

# 6

## Unfinished book on Consent Play

### from A Letter From A Stranger, 1994

In October 1994 I wrote my experience with consent play in a notebook, with the intention of publishing it one day, but I never finished it.
This is what I wrote about my consent play and my affair or relationship with Bear.

### Monday 21- Tuesday 22 October, 1994
### 0.40

I don't know how many words will go into this journal before it's full, how many pages before this ballpoint is empty, or how many stories I need to tell before I have said what I've come here to say, but I do know the limited resources will work in my advantage.

On top of the boundaries set by the material, there is the slowness of it, the thoughts that just drip onto the paper word for word, a little pause at the end of every sentence.
And I've set myself a time limit.
Not because I'm in a hurry finishing or publishing it but because I believe this unspoken confession is what is blocking the pathway to what it is I desire, or who, all of them, the men.

But above all else: Not writing this out is blocking my way to becoming the person I would be in their presence.
The lover who calls herself, yes, what?
What is it, this unnamed role?

Both "girlfriend" and "submissive" are equally misplaced, neither one is what I want to be and at heart already am, just without words so far. How do you name a woman who desires to be in a constant game for her consent?

And not just in the obvious, the play rape.

Although I did think that for a while, that the most defining characteristic of my sexual preference was to be dominated during sex.

But now I know this consent is always played for, and withheld unless I feel I have his full attention, and then we play, I surrender and he can dominate me.

That my desire for power play is weaved into the bigger picture of two lovers only seeing each other for sex, into a date of some sort.

My sexual preference cannot "just" be defined as power play or rough sex, because that would imply that you could be married and have this type of sex at night and then discuss whose turn it is to stock the fridge.

That is not how consent play works- let's call it that for now.

Consent play would ask: What fridge?

What tomorrow?

There is only the now.

It is like a perpetual tango. A game of attraction, where you hope you'll dance again.

There are multiple men I would like to tango with but currently I'm dating none of them.

I don't have to answer to anyone right now, I'm alone with my thoughts and with my desires, between what was and what can become, who I can become.

And when I do the right man will come.

Plural, maybe.

## Tuesday 22- Wednesday 23 October, 1994
## Create the Truth
**0.05**

I tick off the things I want to do each day, cuddle enough with both cats, masturbate, yoga.
Some things are harder than others.
Writing in this journal is also on there and it's one of the things I don't want to skip.
Not even if it's after midnight before I start.

The reason I want to do this is because this activity is called "create the truth";
By writing I want a dominant lover, I will create him.
I need to feel like I am the perfect match and then next to me, like magic, a vacuum will be created that will draw the right man and only the right man, in.

This man will automatically, when we make love, force me down, pin me down, restrict me, push me, command me, open me, enter me, hurt me, fill me, and it will be under that weight that I lean in and let go.

And that I am home.


## Wednesday 23 – Thursday 24 October, 1994
**0.15**

On days like this it's so good to have this diary to come back to.
I didn't do yoga, didn't see friends or a movie. The only thing I did, which was good for my sexuality (or maybe it's more a prerequisite than an aphrodisiac) is deep cleanse my house.
I feel thrilled by this.

I intend to do yoga AM! The PM thing is not working for me. I hope that a sexy yoga session every morning will keep my spirits up for the rest of the day.

That I'll keep identifying with my sexual ambitions, of who I need to be.

Right now I keep forgetting it until suddenly I remember after midnight, when I pick up this journal.

I need to start doing a hell of a lot more to straighten this out, than writing this book.

## Wednesday 30 October, 1994
## A League of their own
## 09.30

First day working from home, and immediately I take this journal and go to the cafe instead of spending the day behind my desk.

Don't worry, I'll make it up.

It's just that I've been in such a dark place that I'm thrilled my desire to journal has returned.

The story has returned.

And it's not the story I thought it was.

Maybe they were related: The story of consent play and my meltdown.

Consent play is a lot more complex than just a variation to S&M.

And I am a lot more complex than just a college grad stuck in her first job.

I may have needed the meltdown in order to do justice to the story, as well as to myself.

Over the past week I've discovered a really big chunk in my identity, that I don't know where to put, or how to interpret it, but it is a place

of strength.
It is about the Catherine Tramell part in me.

Yesterday I was talking about this part to a friend and she said:
"Oh my God, you're sitting just like her."
She was referring to Catherine Tramell, Basic Instinct.
A movie I've seen more than any other.

Just this summer they played it at the discount theater, I went four more times, and I'm thinking of getting a VHS.
After realizing I identify like her, I started wondering where do I behave or feel like Catherine Tramell, if I'm submissive in bed?
If I make myself as grey as possible at work?
Not that I've been very successful at that and I'm glad I can start working from home but nevertheless;
I didn't recognize Catherine Tramell in my submissive sexuality, nor in my bland work life.

I think cutting my personality in half was the biggest cause of me having suicidal thoughts over the weekend.
Not as an act of despair but as a happy thought. A comforting one. One I'd rather thought of than how I was going to solve this.
But the signs that life was slipping though my fingers, had been there earlier.
In no longer masturbating, in no longer writing, and in cancelling appointments.
I had quit eating sugar, which was the first moment death entered my thoughts, as if I wanted to bring my body back to its pre-college thinness before I died.

I felt dead on the inside already and that it needed to stay that way to not disturb the others around me.
The only one who didn't require me to be half-dead already, was Bear.

I have not heard from him in weeks, if not months.

I did run into him and he invited me over or suggested we should see each other soon, but I rejected because if he doesn't want to see me, I don't want him to feel pressured to invite me.

I really believe he has someone else right now.

Meeting up by chance encounter at my all-time low, was out of the question.

On my way home I kept wondering why I had been so determined to reject him helping me.

He had literally offered: "Maybe it helps to talk."

Yet I knew the moment I accepted this, it would not only ruin what we had, but that it was also dangerous because I would become dependent on him.

I would be meeting him from a place of needing him when I want him to want me, not to pity me.

And suddenly I snapped out of it.

I saw why I felt suicidal, why I was so happy with my love life and could even bear the thought of him having someone else.

And where that giant chunk went!

I saw why I had seen Basic Instinct so many times, and why I should buy the VHS.

And most importantly: I saw why my submission during sex was rooted in strength.

My relationship with Bear has been the only place, in all those years, where I have been able to show myself as Catherine Tramell.

He never blinked.

Not when I asked him to become my lover when I was a virgin.

Not when I asked for anal sex.

Not when I asked for play rape.

Playing doctor.

Applauded him for staying sexually active with other women.

Watched him with great love, appreciation and understanding as others around him crashed into his stubbornness.

I saw that we had something that we couldn't have with others because they needed it to have rules, form, agreement, when we had none of those things.

We had a deep understanding and appreciation of each other's strength and independence.

We saw each other as solitary beings, not as half of a couple in need of amalgamation.

My relationship with Bear had been my Catherine Tramell Sanctuary.

And the reason I had been starving myself, denying myself, creatively cutting myself off and ultimately the reason why I wanted to kill myself:

Because in all other aspects of my life I had not been Catherine Tramell.

## Sunday 17 November, 1994
## Epilogue

I just typed out these notes on consent play, and I was right.

This really was, and is, all I can say about it.

Sometimes I think my depression and the current trouble we are going through are the effects of leaving university, and both of us trying to find our place in this world.

I'm convinced we'll stay in touch, over the course of our lives but right now I need to start implementing what I learned about who I want to be.

It's almost 5 years ago that we started our affair, we were both still in high school when we met.

I have become an adult and stepped into my power, but only in my relationship with him so therefor it has been very limited.

You could say I'm only half adult.

Or a part-time adult.

The rest of the time my own power scares me or the response I get from people is starting to scare me.

Now more than ever, it seems.

My studies were filled with male friends, but at the publisher's it's mostly women.

I have definitely not been coping well with that and avoid their company, mostly.


With Bear out of sight, the only place where I've felt good in my own skin, disappeared.

No wonder I feel I'm losing my strength.


Growing up is like shedding skin, isn't it?

You can't enjoy your new identity, if you keep paying attention to everything that has fallen off.

My old life, my student life, is over.

And maybe my relationship with the boy who grew into a man, at my side, is over too.

Maybe our affair is part of the dead skin but maybe it's part of the strong, vibrant beings that we became.

And we'll always keep reinventing ourselves, together.


It reminds me of the final scene of Basic Instinct.


Nick and Catherine just had sex, and Catherine is unsure how they're going to have a normal relationship. She seems terrified and confused, but you can't see if she's having relationship skitters because she's so used to killing the people she loves or if she's scared because everybody

she loves ends up being killed.
Then you think she's reaching under the bed for a weapon, but the movie ends in a passionate kiss, indicating she was never the killer.

Yet after a fade out, Nick and Catherine come back into focus one more time.
This time the camera moves under the bed, where you see an ice pick, indicating she did intend to kill him, and she's the killer after all.
I always thought that last shot was cheap and I didn't buy it.
Not even the first time I saw it.

I didn't buy it that Nick and Catherine would not stay together, since they were a match made in heaven.
No one was playing at their level, and they both had enough experience to know that no one ever would.

Things like that don't end.

*Unfinished book on Consent Play*
from "A letter from a stranger" (diary 1994-1996)

# 7

# "What the fuck do you want from me, Catherine?"

*I feel that the femme fatale figure of legend,*
*myth and modern popular culture*
*tells the truth about sexual relations.*

*About male fear of woman, not male hatred of woman.*

*The femme fatale shows that in her supernatural kind of power,*
*that woman is ultimately unknowable.*

*Not only to man, but to herself.*

*Camille Paglia*
*audio commentary to Basic Instinct*

*This is a letter to my creativity coach Sara.*
*Before our call I always give her a headsup.*

Dear Sara,

There is only one part of my 1994 project that is actually taking flight. Just one part of my life, that easily transcends 25 years back, and I would be able to write about in my 1994 series.
Everything else that happened is just untranslatable.

I can't share that I've decided to go out into the world under my real name, starting with an entirely new Bon Jovi YouTube series.

The only filming we did in 1994, was with a camera that had videotapes in them. And we were unlikely to share it with anyone we did not already know.

I also cannot tell how I found the bestest job in the history of being LS Harteveld.

A job opening which has excited me to the level of Jon Bon Jovi funding my life on the condition that I only do whatever the fuck I want, every day, for the rest of my life.

And if that means I will do him, that would be great. But if not he'll still be my biggest fan.

That would be like the Next Best Thing, to finding this job.

But it is so tied to modern culture that I have not found a way to translate it to 1994.

And in this 1994 series, which really feels like ages since last time I wrote for it, I also cannot tell that in order to apply for this job I am supposed to clean up all my blogs at least to some degree, in order to apply.

And also, the absolute daunting task awaited me, of going through both of the YouTube channels (the description boxes) to clean them up, take out any cross-referencing from my secret pen name to my real name, take out all services that I no longer offer, websites that I no longer support and social media accounts that have changed.

And remove everything that I don't want biting me in the ass, when I'm visible or famous under my real name.

Nor did I want anything online which I did not 100% stood by, the moment I was sending out the most important application of my life.

And – and! – Sara, you are not going to believe this;
I can also not work into my 1994 series that YouTube then did the stuff nightmares are made of:
It.
Unedited.
My.
Videos.

Five years of work, trimmed endings, cut monologues, ringing doorbells and bare bellies from tops that exposed me;
All online.
And that's just the stuff under my real name.
God knows what I edited from my more candid LS Harteveld channel.

That channel could have an atomic bomb of bloopers, that could blow up any career, let alone the carefully crafted public image I was creating under my real name.

But the good news is that the unexpected YouTube fail left me no choice but to simply take down all 500 videos on my two channels, only leaving a goodbye video on my LS Harteveld channel, and the three videos I had shot for my new series under my real name.

It cost me four hours of intense anxiety and full-blown panic on a Monday night.
It saved me days and days of editing description boxes and a guilt trip towards my audience for every video I removed.
A simple apology on both my channels, explaining what had happened and why I removed the videos, was all it took.

I think I owe YouTube a big Thank You.

So all these major life events, the decision to become known under my real name, starting a new video series, finding the perfect job opening, and my adventures with my YouTube channel and the blessing that turned out to be, colored the past two weeks.

Yet I did not write anything for the only series that I hold in the highest regard, and that I consider the most pure version of me:
1994.
Where I translate my life into a fictionalized past.

22 Year old Lauren had not moved a finger, in the area of work nor her writing.
And there was really only one aspect where I knew what she had been up to:
She had fallen in love with Michael Douglas.

She had no idea why she had managed to miss him, when she had seen Basic Instinct at the theater, but she had.
And now that she owned a videotape of Basic Instinct, she just couldn't take her eyes off of him.
She was spellbound by his strong, macho on-screen presence. And she was sure the magic was in his voice.
The way he said:
"What the fuck do you want from me Catherine?" while looking straight into Sharon Stone's eyes, up close, sparked a deep longing in her to be with a man again.
To have a man asking her that question, in an almost bored, definitely not impressed with her, way.

Maybe her ex-lover Bear would?
She still thought almost exclusively about him. Even though he seemed to have really left.
But maybe it would be someone else, someone new who would come into her life and possess that same kind of distant cool, that made her feel safe.

Whoever it was, she would recognize him if she saw him. She was sure of it.

And he, would recognize her.

*"What the fuck do you want from me, Catherine?"* was written on 4 February 2020

# 8

## *Well you know I'm wacko*

I'm now at an intake of over one viewing of Basic Instinct a day. And honestly I have no idea where I get the time.

Especially because I've also consistently been doing my mindset work/ listening to Katrina Ruth on YouTube/ live streams on Facebook. So how do I also watch a feature length movie a day?

And it's so addictive, it took me days to replace it with something else. And now that I have (An Inside Job), I've spontaneously created a home study program from all paid courses from Katrina Ruth, which I own.

In other words, it's much more tempting to study marketing and personal development for entrepreneurs, than to watch any other movie than Basic Instinct.

And the strange thing is, it is doing something to me which I cannot explain. I really have no idea. It's like being in love but not knowing with whom. I mean I'm in love with Michael Douglas, who plays Nick Curran, but that doesn't really explain it. This is something else, I'm sure of it.

The last days have been super intense.
On Thursday I felt this high vibe of creating a new channel under my real name, but on Friday I went down the rabbit hole where I had many adventures, some in this world and others just in my head.

And it took a drastic haircut, a stationary haul, hours at the cafe AND creating an entire education out of all Katrina Ruth programs before the voices in my head finally said:

"Okay, we're done. We're still clueless where we're heading but we do know what you will be doing from now on, to get there."
Which didn't make sense, but I took their word for it.

And in my mind I heard the lines detective Andrews said to a suspended Michael Douglas/ Nick Curran, when he comes to Andrews to ask what he has found out about Catherine Tramell's parents:

NICK:  Did you find out about her parents?

ANDREWS: You're on leave, man. You're on psycho leave. I'm talking to a possible wacko here.

NICK: Well you know I'm wacko, Sam, what'd you find?

They were right. It's not about being wacko.
It's about what you find out.

*Well you know I'm wacko*
was written on 17 February 2020

# 9

## The Rise of Catherine Tramell

*This is a letter to* my creativity coach Sara
*Before our call I always give her a headsup.*

Dear Sara,

Forgive me Father, for I have sinned.
The flesh is weaker than the conscious mind.
Where flesh stands for still following the news day after day, despite making daily resolutions to stop following the news entirely.
And where flesh stands for writing an entire blogpost – twice!- about my real thoughts on Covid.

But before I get to the tricky part, of writing about Covid without creating things I delete, I want to first get back to the part where I changed my mind.
After my last letter to you.
My intention was to stop living so hermit-like, and go out more.
Take more risks.

I was so sick of staying within my (social) boundaries, and could not stand the thought of living in fear of well "people" I think.
Not fear of the virus, just to be clear.

I knew this "daring" new lifestyle would probably cost me my productivity. That I would be so out of whack every time I had seen a friend who had a cold, or had been in a car with someone who then got tested the week after and so on;
And yet, it was worth it.

Then fuck being productive.
Or so I thought.

But reality was a lot more stubborn than just a rational decision to stop being such a pussy, and rock that social life.
Time and time again I was caught off-guard, and I think I now know why;
Because you know what, Sara?
Most people SAY they live according to Covid regulations.
AND THEN THEY DON'T.

So this is what the world looks like to me Sara:

FIRST , "they", society, science, all the scared people, all the dutiful entrepreneurs and organizations, all the healthcare professionals who had to deal with so much death and so on, they tell me Covid is a real threat and that therefor there are these rules in place.

THEN, "they", society, science, all the scared people, all the dutiful entrepreneurs and organizations, all the healthcare professionals who had to deal with so much death and so on, do not obey their own rules.

AND!
The other half of society, alternative news channels, and people who are less scared, the entrepreneurs and organizations who are less dutiful and everyone else who did not have to deal with all the deaths and sick people, also don't obey them because they don't believe it's a real threat.

In other words:
I'm living in a world where from the people who have not stayed indoors for 6 months;
No one obeys the rules.
Half of them despite endorsing them.

They go out coughing, share hand towels, equipment, food, elevators, cars.

They do not keep a 1,5 meter distance, or meet indoors without having any reason to believe the place has some kind of premium ventilation technique.

And yet at the same time, with half of them, it is NOT because they do not endorse the rules;
But it is because unlike me, they never had to internalize what hygiene is, because they were never aids phobic.

My estimate is that unless you're a surgeon, you're not going to understand surface and air contamination.
Because if you did, you would immediately see that the preventative measures may be more than a drop in the ocean;
But they're far from safe or sterile circumstances that will prevent you from getting anything.

And that is IF you obey the rules.
Which like I said: I have (hardly) seen anyone doing, not consistently at least.

So here I was, for the past 6 months, in a world where half of the population endorse the rules and don't diligently follow them, and the other half who do not endorse the rules and also don't follow them. And yet I have been feeling like the villain for concluding that apparently the rules only have the function of giving the impression that "something is being done".
They should make people FEEL safe, when even if the rules would be executed perfectly, they are far from safe.
As the surgeon and the woman recovering from an aids phobia would have been able to tell you.

Yet this whole "playing by the rules" act has been my MO for the past 6 months, and I was like: "Whatever. I'll sit this one out, and I'll cope." But at the back of my head, still, there was this voice that it wasn't about following the rules;

It was about not catching or spreading Covid.

Which if it is as contagious as they say it is, means you cannot do anything where you touch the same surface as someone else, nor go indoors anywhere.

A situation that was only facilitated during the lock down, although our stores stayed open.

For the past 6 months I have not been stressed out by the rules, but by knowing that the rules are not enough to keep it from spreading. As long as the supermarket, the plane or the movie theater are not clean enough to have an open heart surgery, you can still catch Covid there.

That's how I see it.


In the first months I felt angry, but eventually it died out.

And I became apathetic.

I was checking the news sites (sinning) but basically all I did was checking if there were any signs of land.

If there was hope.

And the reason it was so bad for my mental health was because I realized this would stay until at least mid 2021 if not longer.


I've deleted another four paragraphs of medical information; Suffice to say, I have not been able to combine my Covid related stress with giving myself nor my cats the right medical attention.


And it was something that was recently added onto that "I'll sit this one out" pile of delayed medical attention for my entire household (me and the kitties), combined with the six month emotional roller coaster of reading dreadful Covid related news, and being freaked out by many

social interactions, that sparked a new thought;
"What if it *never* goes away?"

What if the conditions that are causing so much anxiety in my social life, and that have made me decide to avoid medical care, are permanent?
What if social distancing stays indefinitely?
What if Covid testing is here to stay, like Chlamydia?
What if a cure for Covid doesn't come until 2034 just like the one for aids/hiv didn't come until 1994;
And there will never be a workable vaccine but only something like Prep, for those at risk of getting Covid?
Then what?

And everything fell into place.
It was the breakthrough I had been looking for.

Of course I wasn't going to watch the news anymore, now that I realized that it may very well stay like this for the upcoming decade and a half.
Just like gay men in the 80s, we might be in for a very long haul.
For the first time in months, I immediately knew what to do.

I sent an email to my dentist and the VET, both explaining my issues with the current situation as well as asking or suggesting ways how we could pick up treatment (safely) for myself (dentist) and the cats (VET).
For now I will keep my ban on the GP and specialists, but I've more or less always had that.
Dental care and the VET are really the only forms of health care that are "aligned" for me.

It's not that it's going to be easy, or immediately solved or anything. But I felt very empowered to pick those ones up, instead of postponing it to some unforeseen future.

And finally The Vision came, of who I am becoming.
And this was also something that had been dangling in and out of focus, for a very long time. It was as if I just couldn't fully grasp it. Or was afraid to leap.
Until now.

In the 1992 movie Basic Instinct, Sharon Stone plays Catherine Tramell.
And although right off the bat, I was totally into her, she also seems to be perpetually growing on me.

Catherine Tramell is not just the type of woman who I think I truly am, and the only writer I have ever really felt connected to;
She also embodies the "role" I feel I currently have, in society.

She's the one who everybody believes to be evil, when she's really not evil at all.
Just strong, misunderstood, and refusing to explain herself.

Identifying with her is my ticket "out of here".
Where "here" is after six months of playing by the rules and missing out on all the fun. And health care.

Basic Instinct, as I see it now, contains an alternative story or theme, that was recognized by at least one other person at the time!
By Sharon Stone herself.

On the special edition dvd, she speaks favorably about her character Catherine Tramell, and the story of Basic Instinct.
Yet last week I heard her talking about her background research for

Catherine Tramell (in interviews for Netflix series Ratched) and it was almost as if she looked back at Catherine Tramell as really having committed the murders.

As really being a serial killer.

I thought:

"She's lost "her"! Even Sharon Stone no longer remembers who Catherine Tramell really was."

Maybe I misunderstood the interview she gave last week or the interview on the 1992 recording.

But Sharon Stone seemed to no longer support a more favorable version, which she offered in that interview from the early 90s. That Basic Instinct was *a love story*.

And this is how I see that story:

Catherine Tramell and Nick Curran, were both fascinated by playing mental games.

I am reading the book for the first time, and Catherine is explained like this;

*"Writing teaches you how to lie," she said crisply.*

*Oh, Jeez, thought Gus, all the ice was thin around this woman. Every word she uttered was loaded with some double meaning.*

But what was too much for Gus, was exactly right for Nick Curran; *He was looking forward to see how much she could be pushed –and how she would push back.*

Nick and Catherine played together because no one else understood the game.

Catherine was not violent, not in a physical sense. But she did have a fascination for people with a history of violence.

Like Nick.

An incident where he had shot two tourists when he had been undercover, had made Nick Curran emotionally wounded and reckless. He was always drawn to violent situations. As if he longed to be punished for what he had done.

For the mistakes he had made.

Or, as his partner Gus called it, Nick felt so guilty that he "tried to wiggle his way into an ice pick".

So I do not see Catherine Tramell as a killer;

But she was surrounded by them.

She sought their company and seemed to have given them ownership over who they were...

Roxy could accept she had killed her brothers.

Hazel Dobkins could accept she had killed her family.

Nick could accept he killed "those tourists".

And all three did those things, long before they met Catherine.

Her presence, her willingness to look them in the eye and be able to be with them despite or maybe even because of what they had done; It's what drew them towards her, as if for one brief moment, they didn't have to carry that burden alone.

But Beth Garner, who studied at Berkley at the same time as Catherine did and who became San Francisco's police psychologist?

She could not cope.

In all probability; Beth Garner was no killer, until she met Catherine and lost her sanity.

Yet Beth Garner was viewed as the "good" one.

In the final scenes of the movie, it is revealed that Beth was the killer, of Johnny Bozz, and of detective Nilsen to whom she gave Nick's psychiatric file;

She killed Gus, and in all likeliness also their mentor at Berkley and her own husband.

But because of one final shot, with an ice pick under Catherine and Nick's bed, it is also ambiguous if all that was true.

To this day director Paul Verhoeven, and now apparently even Sharon Stone herself, claim it was Catherine Tramell, not Beth Garner, who killed Johnny Bozz, Nilsen and Gus.
And then Catherine would also have to be the one who killed the mentor, and Beth's husband.

In my opinion: She wasn't.
It really was Beth.

She got into a deep identity crisis from meeting Catherine Tramell and as a response to not being able to really connect with Catherine and feeling inferior to her, Beth "became" the evil she accused Tramell of. But that was never there.

In 1992, I didn't know the two story lines, both that Beth did it and that Catherine did it, had both been fully developed.
So naturally, I thought if you would dissect the movie, or if I had paid more attention, I would have seen who had "really" done it. I left the theater with the ending that Beth Garner had done all the killing, but nevertheless Catherine had an ice pick under the bed. Which she ultimately did not use, she didn't kill Nick.

Frustrated, I asked my then boyfriend what that ending meant. If Beth had done it, why did Catherine have an ice pick and had considered using it on Nick?
I will never forget what my boyfriend said, and especially now that I know the movie is so complicated, I think he gave the best explanation of the movie I have ever heard:

"Maybe she was so used to having the people around her being killed, that when the killer was caught she felt she had to do it herself."

And that's why I know, this crisis will never be over.
If the virus is gone (the killer is caught), we will be so used to having it around us, that we'll either keep it around by our thoughts, refusing to let it go.
Or we'll create a new enemy thought.
Ten days ago one of the major news sites had three articles on legionnaire's disease;
Maybe that will be the new enemy if Covid is behind bars.
Maybe that will be the ice pick under our beds we're tempted to use because we're so used, and attached, to having death and mayhem around us.

The movie made me see that there is no right or wrong in this crisis. There are multiple story lines which you can follow, and they're all complete.
The whodunnit from Covid will, just like Basic Instinct, always be a matter of preference.

Do you want to believe the good doctor Beth Garner was set up by the *femme fatale*?

Or do you want to believe that the mysterious writer Catherine Tramell just decided to play along?

*"I don't make the rules, Nick. I go with the flow."*

After six months of pretending to be a Beth Garner, I realize I chose the wrong part.
I'm changing my position, and picking up the Catherine Tramell part, just like I have done for years.
My three websites, my three blogs of the past ten years, are filled with

blogs just like this one. Where I realize there is a part of me that has only been represented by her.
A very big part.

But I think I knew even earlier. I think I chose right there in 1992, who I wanted to become, or perhaps had always been.
Her.

I don't make the rules, Sara.

I go with the flow.


~Lauren
*An Unexamined life Is Not Worth living*

*The Rise of Catherine Tramell*
was written on 20 September 2020

# 10
## The Queen of Stinson Beach

*This is a letter to my creativity coach Sara*
*Before our call I always give her a headsup.*

Dear Sara,

First of all;
This post could have, and probably should have, had the title:
"10 Steps That Made Me A 7-Figure Rock Star."
If you see which previously used addition to that title I left out, I'm
giving you extra bonus points.
As if you needed any, after responding to my ten minute story about
being obsessed with the not-known-by-anyone town of Stinson on our
last call, with:
"I know Stinson – "
And giving me your personal memories of it!

But in my enthusiasm to turn this into a game with extra points, I'm
getting ahead of myself!

So, back to where we left off during our last call;
I've since replaced the cover photo of my Twitter and Facebook, to the
Stinson shoreline. A photo tied to the movie Basic Instinct, and one I
will never be allowed to use as the cover for my book:
*C. Stories about cinema, Covid and Catherine Tramell*

In my last email I was talking about "C." as just being my 2020 (Covid)
diary. But shortly before our call, or on the call, I realized the "C." –

which already stood for Catherine Tramell and Covid – could also stand for "Cinema".

Immediately giving the book a wider perspective from a diary of this Covid year, to a collection of stories about Covid and about Catherine Tramell, such as these letters to you and all the other posts I've written about Catherine Tramell and Basic Instinct in the past.

And finally C, standing for cinema, would include stories inspired by movies I saw.
I think I have up to twenty posts, all "Metas" to movies in one way or another.
Out of the top of my head, I remember writing many of them about Star Wars The Last Jedi, a few on the movie Mother, but also on Words of Love, the documentary on Leonard Cohen and Bohemian Rhapsody, which I saw 15 times total.

Turning "C." from a diary into a collection of stories, was actually so freeing that it has made me determined to do all books like that. Leave the idea of publishing my blog posts in the diary format, but curate them around certain topics.
If, in the end, I find that I also have a diary I want to publish, for instance my 1994-1995 project, I can still do that.
But the idea of first focusing on smaller complete series, such as "The Mistress Speaks", or collection of stories around a topic, makes the task at hand so much lighter.

I'm still committed to publishing all my new books in the remainder of 2020.
Despite....

The headaches!
As I'm typing this, Saturday afternoon, I've only just recovered from headaches.

And according to this new 10 Step schedule on how to become a 7-figure Rock Star, I should be taking it easy, and do my yoga and journaling before I dive into the writing.
But I'm just way too excited to not immediately jump into it!

And I mean- what if the headache returns, and I have not written you before our call?
So although I believe there is purpose and point in following the 10 steps, in the right order;
Let's not overestimate my ability to follow them.

The reason I didn't title this post "10 Steps that made me a 7-Figure Rock Star", is because it would be way too self-helpy, click baity and then the post being too wordy to satisfy the hungry visitor.
Best to give it a neutral title;
Stinson Beach.

The two other titles I considered before settling for "Stinson Beach" were:
"The little fellas with the knitting pins who stick them in my head, are back"
But I didn't want to acknowledge my headaches, to the extend that I was now either suffering from them OR writing about them!
Don't want to encourage those little fellas.

And the other title I considered was; "Straight Outta Stinson". Which I REALLY liked, but since I never watched the documentary Straight Outta Compton, nor ever listened to NWA, I found that title too was too click baity too and not be delivering content for someone coming in from that angle.

I just looked it up and in 2010 Stinson Beach had a population of 632. It's a quiet town and the only things ominous about it are the always present fog over the sea, and the great white sharks who have gotten

the town into "The Red Triangle";
And area with a high number of shark attacks.
Stinson is as far from LA rap music and culture as you could possibly get.

So the title became plain and simple;
Stinson Beach.

The small town that you knew from personal experience, and that I had turned into my newest special interest. Me; A woman from The Netherlands, who has never been to California or even in the entire West of the US ever!

Because of the headaches I have not written anything, since my last letter to you. And I've also not watched movies, nor listened to music. I have been doing a training from Katrina Ruth "Identity", plus doing her longer free training videos on YouTube, which she uploaded from 2016 tot the beginning of this year;
But even they are just too potent!
I have them (taking her training) on my 10 Steps schedule, but they're in the final lap. They're for when I feel really strong, and I can let her powerful message fuel me without breaking into bits.
As I have been suffering from lately.

Now just to be clear: I did not get headaches from watching Katrina Ruth, although I am aware it may seem that way.
I got headaches from my request for psychological help backfiring, a situation about which I probably should have filed a complaint with healthcare inspection but I didn't want to invest anymore time in it. And after this had settled, a doctor who also works at my GP office contacted me with new addresses to getting help.
Something I declined but it did result in more stress.

And we also had another Covid related press conference, which was from all the press conferences the most inconsistent one of all. This time they had an entire schedule which they called a "Covid road map" which turned out to be neither a road map (it did not get you to where you wanted to go) nor was it a consistent schedule with regard to which measures would au-to-ma-ti-cally (I presumed!) follow a certain level of having Covid in our communities.

Two days in, the state website claimed the road map was regional when at the press conference the word regional, had not been mentioned even once.
What had been presented was a bunch of NATIONAL measures (which were not even on the road map) and this ->unspecified <- roadmap. A national roadmap, one assumes.
The state website showed it had presumably been a regional roadmap, all along.

In case you're wondering "Isn't The Netherlands too small for a regional road map?"
Yes.
It's bollocks.
This road map will never be used because as soon as there is any trouble, national measures will be taken.

However in theory you could use a regional road map for national Covid measures if you would said f.e. ;
"We're setting the entire country on level 3. This means that all measures for level 3 will now be applicable for the whole nation."

I really thought – and I can only say I was so naive here;
I thought that – and I had actually already printed it, because I was convinced it could not mean anything else!
I was convinced I would ONLY need this new road map from now on.
Level 3?

* looks at the road map *
* sees column with measures level 3*
Got it!

When in reality, we got national measures, with a name ("partial lockdown") that was not referring to a certain level nor name used on the card.
And the new set of measures were not found in one column but either not mentioned on the map, or scattered throughout like confetti.

A cluster fuck Sara, that's what it was.

JUST when I thought I could finally let out a sigh of relief, that they had bettered their ways and had something which would free us from constantly having to tune in to all the changes.

Yet no one seemed to mention, seemed to care, and an entire parliamentary debate went by without someone roasting it.

I hate roasts done for fun. But for this ill-equipped road map plan I think a proper roast was the only appropriate response.

Oh!
And one of the things they will very soon find out, is that if they indeed intend to use our emergency Covid legislation in order to make non-medical mouth masks mandatory?
Dutch legal experts will have them raw.

Because this law states that citizens can be forced to wear;
"Personal protection"
Covering your mouth with "something"? Is not personal protection!
A condom, is personal protection.
A real medical mask, is personal protection.

Non-medical masks offer at best some protection for other people, and they appear courteous.

The emergency Covid legislation should have stated that the government can make people comply with symbolic measures, that might be ineffective or even counter effective "but that most people get a safe feeling from".
In that case, they would be able to get the mandatory mouth masks through in 10 minutes.
But based on personal protection?
They'll have them raw, Sara.

And although I'm all pro-etiquette and don't mind wearing a face mask at all, I look forward to the legal massacre this mouth mask legislation is going to be.

I give Dutch politicians heading for mandatory mouth masks, the survival chance of a surfer with an open wound on his leg, peddling his board in The Red Triangle of Stinson Beach.
I read they pulled one out who needed 600 stitches.

So after my Monday, Tuesday, and Wednesday being lost to seeing my personal chances of getting the correct psychological help evaporate (after my medical data were leaked – It was a minefield!) and lost them to getting worked up about the inconsistency of Dutch Covid regulation;
My Thursday had a high pulling myself up by the bootstraps level!

I called it my day of Rebirth, and I was determined to never let myself be pulled into the shark infested waters of getting psychological help.

Nor was I ever going to invest in understanding which contradictory, bullocks plan our government was selling this time.
Not even when it seemed like a good and sound plan, because the

disappointment that it was yet another road map to absolutely nowhere, made it all the more painful.

And it worked.
Thursday was A Milestone Day!
By the time it had finished I felt really good, and I had made some really big improvements to my house.
Most notably I now have a cozy yoga corner in the warmest room of the house, my study.
Now that it's winter the living is always a bit colder, and sometimes the cats want the balcony door open, so this is much better.

And then Friday came.

Now, throughout the entire week I had been taking Katrina Ruth training, and on most days it was the only thing I felt really confident over.
In the midst of all the craziness, focusing on personal development and what I want for my art and my life, were the moments I felt Life mattered and that it was more than being played by medical professionals and our government.

But even Thursday, I could already sense studying Katrina Ruth was starting to take up too much time in the morning – often up to two hours for one 45 minute video.
And that it didn't result in me writing, nor publishing my books – which was going to be my main goal for 2020.
Thursday was my "regroup" day, so to speak.
I could count that as being "lost", to needing recovery time for all the anger and frustration I had felt at the beginning of the week.

But Friday was the first day I could have done something "real".

Maybe that is why on Friday I noticed it more, how intense studying Katrina Ruth was. And when I developed a headache and ultimately had to go to bed to recover, I knew I needed more of a plan to my life than "refrain from news" and "don't talk to doctors".

Which is when I developed the 10 Steps that are going to make me a 7-Figure Rock Star – period!
LOL
The missing word was "writer".
But you knew that right?

I used to see myself, or maybe "seeing myself" was not the right word, but the closest definition of myself and what it is I do, is "Writer".
Hence:
7 Figure Rock Star Writer.

But from taking all the Katrina Ruth training – and I don't even remember when it clicked exactly – but from studying with her, I knew I had to ditch the "writer" part.
For many reasons.
(oh, and I cried, it was an emotional moment when in my head, I crossed out , and became a Rock Star)

The first reason I crossed out writer is because when Covid is over, I want to spend as little time writing or behind my desk as possible. I've made jokes I do not want to spend even one night in my own bed! Wouldn't that be something?
Either way, being known as "a writer" is setting myself up for doing something I no longer want to do.

Secondly because I feel yoga is such an integral part of who I am. I don't feel I am a yoga teacher in the traditional sense, anymore. But months ago, I already had a calling. Just like Joan of Arc that kind of

level:
"Yoga is my art"

Since then I still have no idea how this would be possible, but I know this is true.
Yoga, not writing, is my art.
But Rock Star Yoga Teacher also didn't had the right ring to it, but neither did Rock Star Writer, since there was too much yoga "in me".

Thirdly, and this is the thing we had a lot of fun with in our last call, was that I feel that since Jon Bon Jovi has basically stepped down from the stage, and sees himself more as a writer, a singer songwriter, a recording artist, and only as a touring musician/ performer last; I feel there's a Rock Star vacancy.

There's no one guarding the stage.

He didn't leave the stage in so many words, but if he is vocal about seeing himself as a writer, and applauded by critics for having delivered such a timely, and relevant singer/songwriter album?
That stage is free.

I know because I was a writer for fourteen years, and that is not the stage.
I feel 2020, with him becoming a writer and me publishing all my books before the end of the year so that I am free to perform and take the stage;
There is an energy of roles being reversed, or switched.

Because that was the second "calling" I got:
I know I am a performer.
The whole list of incomprehensible "calls" is:
1. Get in front of as many people as possible

2. Yoga is my art
3. Album, tour. Album, tour.

This is ALL I have to go by.
And I understand some of them a little bit, and none of them fully.

Three incomprehensible clues about a life that I do not know yet.

And writing not being a visible part of it, as 1, 2, or 3.

Writing is "not on the map".

* silence *

* hears penny drop *

That's when I suddenly knew what my plan was going to be!

First of all, I was going to drop the title "writer".
I no longer feel that emotion, but I know I got emotional when I saw I was ready to go next level, and to no longer "be" a writer. And it was my real name.
This is my pseudonym blog, but my future as a non-writing Rock Star is under my real name.

And the second insight, which was not emotional at all, was that I was going to write out a road map to become a 7-Figure Rock Star. My new identity, without "writer".

And after being so angry over all the mistakes our government had made in drawing up their Covid road map, I knew exactly what a GOOD road map looked like!

* fast forward one day *

It's Sunday night now.
The day I would have finished this blog post, and the moment I would have shared my 10 step system.

So here we are, one day after I logged off because I had been writing for 5 hours straight.
And feeling like a totally new person.

Yesterday, I was so happy I finally knew how to regulate my emotions.
By limiting my time online.
By not writing before I had done my journaling.
By not studying Kat before I had done everything else.

And by putting sex and men at number 10 – yes, they were at ten on my list!

And yet by the time I went to bed?
I had broken ALL the rules.
Written you.
Not done yoga.
Binged on Kat.
And met a man.

And yet I did not have a headache, and I felt better than I had in weeks!

I couldn't sleep, I was definitely overstimulated. Because I had met someone online, who I know NOTHING about. Technically I don't even know if it is a "he".
And yet....
I do.

It's a "he".
A him.

I don't know his age, but I know a few of his friends (maybe that's why I know he's male too) and they are way younger than I am. So that's why I think he's younger.

It's so strange because this is the first time I meet someone in a "setting" that is mysterious;
We know very little about each other.
Just a common interest, or experience, that connects us.
But like I said, there seems to be something else...

And meeting this man changed EVERYTHING.

The entire 10 step plan that was going to ensure that I didn't get all stressed out by men and stress, pretty much received its death verdict, when this man, in one of our first moments of conversations, made a bold move;
At EXACTLY the right time, Sara!

It bore the markings of a chess player, knowing exactly what he did. Deliberately moving the horse towards the Queen.

Would The Queen move to the back of the board, to the sides, or would she move towards him?
Every move would tell him something about her.

I now know the title of this blog post:
Not "Stinson Beach".
It will be "The Queen of Stinson Beach".

And I'm betting my Bon Jovi collection, he'll "get" that.

Was it a coincidence?
That on the Saturday night I wrote for 5 hours straight, determined to finish this post today and describe my list with 10 points;

That EXACTLY on that night, things picked up between a stranger and me?
Someone I have never met before?

But someone who does, what no one before, during or after my lover had been able to do.

Play...

Have I ever told you why I knew that in 1992, Sharon Stone knew the essence of the movie Basic Instinct, where all the other people insisted on having a simplistic view of "her" character being a killer?

The interviewer asked her what the movie was about and she answered:

"It is a love story."


~Lauren
*An Unexamined life Is Not Worth living*




*The Queen of Stinson Beach*
was written on 18 October 2020

# 11

## The Erotic Space Between Catherine and Nick

By now I know more about the meaning of the movie Basic Instinct, than the people that created it.

Originally, just like most people, I thought there was some kind of hidden secret. A whodunit Easter egg or clue we all missed, that would explain the entire movie.

Now this blog post is not at all about if Catherine Tramell, the female protagonist (some would argue the antagonist) is the murderer or not, but maybe it does help to know that I have concluded that she is not. Which allows me to watch this movie entirely as a love story between the writer and 103 million rich Catherine Tramell, and the San Francisco police detective Nick Curran, who has a shady past where he went rogue doing undercover work.

She has been studying Nick to model the main character for a new book she is writing.

The book is called "Shooter", after Nick's nickname. He shot innocent bystanders on a drug bust.

Presumably when he was on coke.

This was the time Nick was pulled out of his undercover work, and had to face charges, making headline news.

This was also the time when he must have caught the attention of Catherine, and she started investigating him for a new book.

If we look at Basic Instinct as a love story between a writer who is falling in love with her main character, and a troubled detective who

has even lost his wife to suicide in the wake of the charges but whose spirit is unbroken;
Then this story becomes even more compelling than if you focus on the brutal murders taking place.

You see that the brutal murders serve as the backdrop, it is the stage where Catherine and Nick find each other.
And because they are the only two people who are not intimidated or scared by the murders taking place, they immediately recognize each other as kindred spirits.
They are both familiar with death, and have both been in a dance with danger their entire lives.
But there is something else;
They both live in their own space.

They live in the world between worlds.

Last week when I started this blog, I did it because I realized I was more fascinated with the (inner) world where the art is created;
Than with the craft of the fine arts themselves.
It also explains my preference for immaterial art in the form of performance art of Marina Abramovic as well as the music and concerts from Bon Jovi.
A remarkable difference between Marina and Jon Bon Jovi is however, and I don't know if you've noticed this, that Marina seems to carry her world between worlds, her space as an artist, with her all the time.
Just like Madonna, or Obama.
They're always "On".
Whereas Jon Bon Jovi does not do that, and is often very laidback and usually more concerned with his philanthropy projects than with being in his artistic space on a day to day basis.
For him the artistic space is related to actively performing on stage, to writing music, to singing;
But it's not where he lives.

But Catherine Tramell from the movie Basic Instinct lives in her artistic space.

She creates her own life with the dynamics, and topics she's interested in. She actively scouts interesting people, she can write about. Exactly like she did with Nick.

"How's your book coming around?" Nick asks at some point.

"It's practically writing itself," she answers, referring to all the things that are happening in Nick's life.

She only has to write it down.

And Nick too, lives in his own space. His is a space of danger and adventure. Catherine deliberately creates her own space, the stage for her books; But Nick is more someone who is drawn to worlds that already exist, and then is a master player in them.

He is aware of the space, the world between worlds, which gives him an advantage.

Most people take life very seriously, and do not see that they are free to choose their own part.

To choose who they want to be.

To switch or uplevel their character.

Nick does.

But Catherine?

She's the one who first conducts the play, who orchestrates its elements, and then waits for her characters to start playing. Most play without knowing it, think what they see in her is reality.

Unlike all of Catherine's friends, unlike her former partners and unlike the retired rock n roll star named "Johnny" and his surname starts with a B (I'm not making this up!);

Nick plays deliberately.

Catherine and Nick immediately recognize each other;
They both live in the world between worlds.
In the world behind our own world.

And when everybody else is worrying about murders taking place, and subpoenas, and warrants, and drama and mayhem;
All they see is each other.

Those of us who visit the world between worlds, to create their art or create their lives, know you are almost always alone there.
Marina meets others there when we are part of her exhibition.
Jon meets us there when he is on stage, and we are in the audience.

But Nick and Catherine, were eye to eye, privately.
They really saw only each other. There was a whole layer of reality between them, that others could not enter.

The first time I consciously started toying with the idea of what I have now called the world between worlds, was when I heard Esther Perel's talks on creating erotic space between long-term couples.
She defines it as a space of possibilities and adventure.

But what I have experienced is that some people carry this space in themselves. And they create their art, or their relationships, from there. You enter their play, just like you see their rock show, or visit their exhibition.
I believe this is a factor in being sexually attractive (or active) that I have not heard about before;
If you live or visit this other world, artistic space, erotic space. If you are a creator of worlds just like Catherine.
Or if you are an active player in that space, like Nick.
Yet dividing the roles this strict is not how it is;
They're both players.
And they're also both creators of this world, with their consciousness.

In the world between worlds there is no difference between the creator and the created.
Between the player and the played.
It is a place where everything is possible, but the price for being there is that you need to give up your idea of right and wrong, and of reality.

Like wanting to know who did it in Basic Instinct.

*The Erotic Space Between Catherine and Nick*
was written on 19 January 2021

# 12

## *Road Map To Success Received. Over.*

*"I'm a writer, I use people for what I write.*
*You write what you know.*
*Let the world beware."*

*Catherine Tramell*

*This is a letter to my creativity coach Sara.*
*Before our call I always give her a headsup.*

Dear Sara,

When I was looking for a new photo of rock star writer Catherine Tramell from Basic Instinct, to go with this post, I could not help but wonder:
"Why am I making this so complicated?"

Why do I switch from calling myself a rock star writer, to rock star artist, simply rock star (in a brave attempt to be done with the issue), to rock star creator?

Only to end up on Sunday 28th March, eagerly writing you ten days before our usual date, because I feel I have such big news! "I am a writer Sara! I'm certain of it!"

It's either writing you this early debriefing or tattoos, Sara.

Either I try to grasp this truth, by ingraining it into my very soul. Or I get tattoos: "I am a writer! I am a writer! I am a writer!" covering my entire body.

And because I'm attached to keeping my skin as it is, after not getting tattooed age 16 because I could not choose between a skull on my upper-arm or a tribal at my lower back, I'm not getting the tattoo.

In hindsight it's a good thing I didn't get those tattoos, because the correct choice at the time was the tribal on my lower back because it was original and very aesthetic.

Except that was 1988.

Ten years later half of female Netherlands had one, yet the skulls-to-upper arm tattoos are to this day reserved for a small and conspicuous group!

The reason I already knew of the tribal lower back tattoos way before anyone else did, was because I was subscribed to a magazine, Revu, which was catered to a male audience. It had a lot of reports on crime, interviews with famous men (mostly) and leaned heavily on photography.

One of their photographers was Patricia Steur, who was good friends with Henk Schiffmacher who also worked at Revu and may be the most famous tattoo artist of the world.

I'm not really sure because I once saw a documentary on a former Amsterdam brothel Yab Yum, and the documentary contained a 90s clip that it was the most expensive club/brothel of the world and it struck me how little fact-checking could be done in the 90s.... With this story about Steur and Schiffmacher taking place in the 80s, I have no idea who was the most famous tattoo artist then!

But Patricia Steur worked with Henk Schiffmacher at this magazine, and he was the one who brought these tribal tattoos from the Maori into his work.

So that is why Patricia had one of the first lower back tribal tattoos of the world.

I can't remember on which photo in Revu I saw her tattoo, but I do remember telling for decades after, how I almost got one of those tattoos, because in the 80s Patricia Steur had one.
So that's how I know it was her!

So, no tattoos again, but I do hope to remember for the rest of a life:
I AM A WRITER!

Even though I have called myself Rock Star * something *  for ages.

So before this morning's epiphany, I was a Rock Star *Creator*. Which I have been for about four months.
Although "Creator" was, and is, technically true, I knew it didn't have the right ring.

And then I haven't even discussed the 20 years where I identified as a yoga teacher!
And since 2015 a Rock Star Yoga Teacher, yes.

But I have discovered that the underlying principle in ALL my work, and also why ALL my titles feel wrong and yucky, is a mindset one.

It is the principle that reality is created by yourself, a concept often referred to as metaphysics.

*Metaphysics is the branch of philosophy that examines the fundamental nature of reality, including the relationship between mind and matter, between substance and attribute, and between potentiality and actuality.*

*Wikipedia*

The great 20th century thinkers I study are often referred to as metaphysical teachers, but I have discovered it is a bit more complicated than that.

Or a lot more complicated.

And that trying to explain to what branch I belong within metaphysics, is only going to complicate matters even further.

It's like if you want to know the nature of the universe you ultimately end up with mostly space and a few atoms flying around in whatever way *you think* they're flying around;

Once I start studying what I do, who I am, hoping to find something solid?

I end up with endless spaciousness and limitless options of what could be true.

Before I wrap this up to how this ultimately has helped me find my way back, just a little word on that metaphysics being the basis from which I operate;

It explains SO MUCH about why I don't get along at all with everyday life!

Because I really feel reality is being created *by us*, because the emotions attached to it are created by us, and therefore, just like the atoms, the truth is shaped not so much based on how *reality* was at t=-1

But at how we responded (usually: freaked the fuck out) at t=-1

So therefor in discussing, or solving a problem existing at t=0 (now), I automatically, I really cannot stop this, start looking at t=-1

"Okay, let's start at the beginning:

Who was energetically connecting with this thing at t=-1?

And who is probably still giving it their undivided negative fear-based attention?"

and:
**What does that person need to stop doing that?**

The professional, teacher, guru, who can leave the first half of the entire equation out, and start treating the situation without addressing that, but instead immediately comes up with something that *automatically* addresses the final part (stops people to worry, and elevates them to start thinking and believing constructively);
That person can save the world.

He or she makes the bad situation now go away without discussing how we got from $t=-1$ to $t=0$ because we thought ourselves that way. The fictional imaginary thoughts that gave an outcome that was perceived as reality (but that were just thoughts about reality), are reversed, by giving a tangible solution or system that will reverse an unwanted $t=0$ back to a neutral $t=-1$.

And since many professionals believe their system, their yoga, their self-help book, their medical treatment, solves the problem; And many people consulting these professionals have faith in these methods; A lot of good is done in this world!
Problems are solved in a natural swift matter, without anybody yelling at the top of their lungs:
"Who let his or her fear-mind run rampant, and worried us all into the apocalypse? Well?"

I would.

And I would be pointing, as if it was pee or poo that someone just dropped in the middle of the living and that I simply refused to clean up, without first coming to an understanding that this is preventable if we all use the toilet.

I don't mind cleaning up poo, I don't mind attending to the ones who are incapable of controlling their bowel movements.

But I am not the person to start normalizing just letting it run all over the place.

However, tackling t=0 problems rarely includes an assessment of t=-1, and how we got from one to the other.

So much for the metaphysical part of this post.

**Am I a metaphysical teacher who writes and speaks about the nature of reality?**
**Absolutely.**
**Am I now going to call myself Rock Star Metaphysical Teacher?**
**Not even at t= one million years.**

So the past couple of weeks I went through a cycle of feeling "I'm almost there!" "I am so close to finally defining what I do!"
Only to end up with out of control atoms, shooting in every direction.

Okay, that was not little..
A little word on metaphysics, right? That's how I announced it. And then it was not little.
This makes it difficult to write this post, as I intended. Because I was going to include the whole process of how I got there, by copying directly from my journal.
I had done 7 journaling exercises to discover my values! Discovering my VALUES is what gave me my big OMG I REALLY AM A WRITER! moment!

It was an exercise I had been wanting to do for some time now. It was as if I knew it (knowing my values) held information that was important. Even to me.

Although even not knowing my values I can't really go against them, effectively.

I just blow things up, if I do something against my values.

But without knowing why, and without knowing beforehand I'm going to blow it up;

So I think my curiosity to know my values was also practical. To make things more pleasant for everybody.

And the exercise went really well.

Because regardless of how broad my likes and dislikes were, as were the things I wanted to change, and as wide as the gap between me and the world seemed (it even included full-blown rants);

They all created a picture that was "Remarkably consistent"!

That was also the alternative title for this post. "Remarkably consistent."

Because if I don't count all my endless deviations where I try so very hard *not* to be a writer, I really am very consistent!

The only thing I really have been doing all the time, is writing. Regardless of how I label it.

I'll take you by the biggest aspects of my values/ life, and how they point to being a writer. And not to anything else, not even a world famous artist/ creator.

Here we go.

VALUE; BEING AT HOME WITH MY CATS

Well, "at home"? After a year of being Covid-confined, I would appreciate a week away now and then, but that doesn't exactly count as "rocking your life and making it big".

Keith Haring didn't spend the last years of his life sitting at home and sending his paintings out on UPS.

Marina lived from a van for years and then had a great wall to climb. And every big artist in history has multiple houses, which they visit in the scarce weeks they are not touring the world.

Staying at home in the world of art, is not really a thing.
Unless?
You guessed it; Unless you're a writer.

A writer is the only person of whom it is accepted that they only visit the real world. Occasionally.

We don't like leaving the house.
Or as Catherine puts it, when Nick Curran and Gus come to her house trying to make her come to the police station voluntarily:
"Read me my rights and arrest me, and I'll go downtown. Otherwise, get the fuck out of here."
There is a silence and she looks at the detectives:
"Please."


VALUE; FREEDOM

Freedom in the broadest sense, for example sexually, creatively and financially.
But that's not exclusive to being a writer, so I'm going to focus on why "freedom" was insufficiently guaranteed by defining myself as a speaker, artist, creator and even "author". Since author means you have a publisher.

The freedom a self-published writer has, that almost no other artist has is:
Not being bothered by contractual obligations!
I did not stop having a company, stop being a business, in order to prevent having to deal with legislation surrounding that (such as

privacy of data, financial administrative obligations, terms of service, liability) to ever allow for even the scent of administrative and communicative obligations, expectations, fine tuning and so on.

I have total freedom to create whatever I want.
And then you are free to pay me because you desire to do so, you can shower me with gifts or you buy from me. Or you don't.
It's that simple.

So it's not that I would not be able to entertain, to enlighten, to surprise, and to charge thousands for a public appearance or make tons of money from a tour.
It's just that I don't want to because I don't want the paperwork, liabilities, and professionalism. The availability to other people's agenda.

I'll just be a writer.
And if you want me to come over?
Then YOU get the paperwork in order and take care of my transportation downtown, offer me coffee, and tell me where to sit.

And then I'll cross my legs and give you a show you'll never forget.


VALUE; BEING IN MY OWN WORLD

Fortunately, this is something many artists value, and many artists get to have!
However for teachers, entrepreneurs, leaders, entertainers, and service providers, "being in their own world" is not on the menu. Their job, the aspect of their work they are paid for, is;
They have to relate to other people.

Non-artists directly have to invest in the relationship with their public, audience, tribe, and actively participate in it.

When I, really, already feel slightly nauseous when I "have to" repost a blogpost I wrote myself, to give it a better exposure, and to be present on social media.

On social media it makes a lot of difference when you post; if you post twice you really do get twice the number of readers. But that already feels, to me, out of integrity. Even though up until now I have done it. I feel I owe it to my work and also readers, when deep down? It is not what I really want. Nor what I feel is in integrity for me.

This feels in integrity to me:
Write whatever I want. Post it. The end.

And on days I do not write (for that account) I still have not found my form in how to communicate, really. How to not be a total jerk on social media, by not showing up unless you have something new; But also stay true to myself and not repost , when I'm really not feeling the same urgency as I did when I wrote the post....

But having said all this, deciding if you "have to" repost your own work, is still VERY different, to what your job is if you have a non-artist job.
Because you are paid to anticipate to what other people think and (most of all) what they need to feel better.
When, as we discussed in my take on metaphysics, that is not my forte.

I do have the empathy to see that everyone who is sad, in trouble, hurt, or just a bit flat and in need of some direction, deserves to be heard, helped, and inspired to do better and to make their life totally rock by some amazing system or show that you have for sale or that you are

going to provide!
Amazing! Keep doing that!

But I'm the person who touches their chin and wonders:
"Really? And what happened before that, at t=-1?"

Or:
"Are you arresting me?"
"Can I change into something more appropriate?"
"Why would I need an attorney?"

I would ask:
"I'm using you for my detective. In my book. You don't mind, do you?"


~Lauren
*An Unexamined life Is Not Worth living*

*Road Map To Success Received. Over.*
was written on 28 March 2021

# About The Beach, C.

The morning detective Nick Curran wakes up, played by Michael Douglas, he finds a note on the pillow next to him.
It reads, in a steady handwriting; the beach C.
And it is from Catherine Tramell, a mysterious writer played by Sharon Stone, with whom he has spent the night.

The beach from the note, refers to her villa in Stinson, a 50 minute drive from the San Francisco mansion, where Nick just woke up after what he called "the fuck of the century".

Although I have loved the movie Basic Instinct (1992) since its release, it took until 2018, when the first posts of this book are dated, before I saw the resemblance between Catherine and me, and that I did have Catherine's cool.
I shock people, even though I do not actively, as in a verb, shock people.
My presence brings an unease that I have spent my entire life, trying to socialize away.
The difference between Catherine and me, was that she did not try to smooth it out and poured some fuel on the fire instead.
It took me until 2018, before I saw my relationship with my lover mirrored her relationship to Nick Curran.
That we shared a love for games, an unavailability to play life at an ordinary level.

It took me until 2018, to understand that my fascination for her had always been way more than a love for stylish clothes and a VIP lifestyle.
That even in 1992, what I had seen in her?
Was me.

# About the cover

*It was a nice day for a ride and a ride to Stinson encompassed a lot of landmarks and beauty spots.*

*The Golden Gate Bridge, then past Sausalito on Highway 101 to Highway 1,*
*the famous cliff-hugging coast road that twisted and curved north.*

*from the book "Basic Instinct"*
*based on the movie*

I was so happy when I found the cover photo for this book, by Adam Derewecki.
It is a picture of Stinson Beach, very close to this "cliff-hugging" road from San Francisco to Stinson Beach.

In the movie, detective Nick Curran is seen driving that road several times, but the two most memorable ones are when he and his partner Gus Moran, take Catherine Tramell from Stinson to the San Francisco police station.
She's directly inspired by Kim Novak's character in Hitchcock's Vertigo; A cool blonde, her hair up, and dressed in a white turtleneck dress and a white woolen coat.
Catherine is sitting at the center of the backseat, often filmed through the rearview mirror, having a conversation with Nick Curran. Filled with double layers.
In order to get the lighting so perfectly hitting her beautiful face, at exactly the right time, Dutch cameraman Jan de Bont had to bend over backwards.

The other memorable scene this road is featured in, is when Nick is following Catherine, who speeds up her Lotus Esprit;
Forcing Nick to dangerously maneuver to keep up, pass other cars on this two lane road with its many corners and not being able to see what's coming.
It almost sends him off the cliff, when an opposing truck comes directly at him.

The road between San Francisco and Stinson Beach, is a natural extension of the character of Catherine Tramell.
It is dangerous and unknowable to others, but whether she's chatting with detectives who are bringing her in, or speeding in her car;
To her that road is home.

All books available worldwide at:

https://www.lulu.com/spotlight/LaurenandLulu

The best book to buy after *The Beach, C.* is

**A letter from a stranger**
diary 1994 – 1996 (to be published early 2022)

Chapter 5 and 6 were a pre-publication from that book.

# The Wait Worth 8 (2017)

1. **Mango**, een novelle *Dutch*
   Seksuele safari, van de jaren '80 tot de zero's.

2. **Dutch American Diary** (2008-2009)
   Lauren is in love with two men;
   One cunning wizard and one half her age.
   ~Dutch American Diary part 1

3. **22 Erotische Verhalen** *Dutch*
   Literaire pornografie in de geest van Anais Nin
   en Isabel Allende.

4. **LS Diary** (2012-2013)
   About three dark men and Lauren getting naked on stage.
   Not necessarily together.
   ~Dutch American Diary part 2

5. **De Candystop** (2013) *Dutch*
   Waar de Nederlandse literatuur tot stilstand komt door een
   Marokkaanse lekkernij.

6. **Bedtime Stories** (2014)
   Facing her demons and her muse, Lauren's sexual history
   gets its worthy finale.
   ~Dutch American Diary part 3

7. **Mirage** (2014)
   Giving you a little dessert, with all gorgeous writers from
   previous books.
   ~Dutch American Diary epilogue

8. **Big**, diaries and erotica (2015-2016)
   The crown to Lauren's life; a secret affair with her Biggie.

# Separate books

These books are not part of the numbered (diary) series

- **Het Boek Benjamin** *Dutch and English*
  Collected works, contains book 1 -8 from the previous page

- **Witte Tijgerin**, *Dutch*
  Gids voor solitaire vrouwen die een geweldig seksleven
  willen en plenty energie.

- **The White Tigress Yoga Workbook**

- **The Mistress Speaks** (2018 -2021)
  Channeling a lost archetype

- **The Beach, C.** (2018 - 2021)
  Diary, letters and essays inspired by Basic Instinct's
  Catherine Tramell

- **Star Wars is finally telling women *cross out* everybody to start enjoying The Thing** (2018 - 2019)
  And other deeply personal blogposts about the sequel trilogy
  that did not age well

- **A Porn Star Love Life** (2015 - 2019)
  stories that brush on, toy with and praise, my love for
  pornography and sex workers